The
Love
Walk

Ziklag Publishers
165-100 Baisley Blvd. Suite 340363
Jamaica, NY 11424

Ziklag Publishers

© 2020 by Claudette Glaude-Scott

ISBN 978-1-7364992-0-7

The Love Walk

Walking in the Power of Love

Devotional

By Claudette Glaude-Scott

DEDICATION

This book is dedicated to my grandmother, Evelyn Glaude, whose life was indeed a Love Walk.

Table of Contents

INTRODUCTION

Wat is love? Everyone has an answer. Some say it's the feeling they have for their spouse and children. For others, it's the feeling they have for their car and home. Today, you see so many atrocities done in the name of love: love of self, love for country, love of ideology. However, the pain those actions inflict on others can never be guided by love.

When you think about love, what do you say?

If you want to know what love really is, you will have to look elsewhere. Love places the well-being of others ahead of its own. Love would give at the cost of life itself to the giver. In the Bible you discover what true love is.

Long ago humanity found itself in a predicament. God created man and placed him in the perfect environment. Everything needed to live a happy and peaceful life was there. God gave man access to every tree in the garden – but one. Man disobeyed and lost his way. Gone was the fellowship that existed between God and man. Gone was the perfect environment for living. However, God's love was greater than man's sin. God found a way to bridge the gap and restore the fellowship lost in the garden.

> *For this is how much God loved the world — he gave his one and only, unique Son as a gift. So now everyone who believes in him will never perish but experience everlasting life.*
>
> (John 3:16 TPT)

Yes, God demonstrated what love is: love gives. The benchmark for love is giving.

Man has tried continually to develop a standard of love outside of God. They believe that good deeds will give them favor with God. But when you try to replace love with good works, it falls short. You cannot understand love without God. God's example of love is your prototype to follow. You have to use the standard set by God to evaluate your love. He set the bar extremely high but it's attainable with His help.

So how is your Love Walk? The Word of God gives clear directives about your walk as it pertains to your love for God and your love for others. I had to examine my Love Walk. This is not a test where you need a score of 75 to get a certificate. You have to attain mastery in all the components to love the way God intended.

In the days ahead, you will have an opportunity to examine your Love Walk through the Word of God. This book also provides practical activities for reflection. As you engage with the Word, you will be able to identify areas of concern and modify your walk so that your journey can be a Love Walk.

GOD IS LOVE

Dear friends, let us continue to love one another, for love comes from God. Anyone who loves is a child of God and knows God. But anyone who does not love does not know God, for God is love.

(1 John 4:7-8)

The Apostle John opened this statement by calling the community together. He began by saying, *"let us continue to love one another."* You know at once that there is activity that he wants and values. In other words, they were engaged in a Love Walk and he wanted the walk to continue.

God created man with the intent of having ongoing fellowship with Him. Man was perfect and God gave Adam His directive for life in the garden. Adam could eat from any tree but one; yet he chose to eat the fruit from the forbidden tree. Adam had to have his own way. So man sinned and destroyed that perfect trusting relationship that first existed with God.

A holy God ejected sinful man from the perfect environment because sin carries a penalty. However, God had a plan to redeem man from his sin. God loved man in spite of his sin and so He demonstrated the perfect example of love. God was aware that Adam's actions in the garden made it plain that he chose to disobey Him. When God came to have a time of fellowship with Adam and Eve, they hid from Him. They were aware of what they had done. Their actions changed the relationship they had with God forever. But God's love was so strong that, even in the process of casting Adam and Eve out of the garden, He promised a redeemer.

That is a demonstration of true love. As the Bible puts it: *"But God showed his great love for us by sending Christ to die for us while we were still sinners"* (Romans 5:8). Jesus walked this earth as man, though sinless, but died the death of a criminal for our sakes to bridge the gap between man and God. He took upon Himself our sin and guilt as a sacrifice so that our condemnation might be transferred to Him.

Bringing Conviction through Love

As one of Jesus' disciples, the Apostle John witnessed the way Jesus exhibited love for those with whom He interacted. In John chapter 4 Jesus met a woman at the well in a Samaritan village, while He and the disciples were on their way to Galilee. The disciples had gone to buy food, so He was alone. When the woman approached, He asked her for water. His request surprised her because there was a history of discord between Jews and Samaritans.

You see, Samaria was part of the northern kingdom known as Israel. The Assyrians had captured Israel and taken some of the people into captivity, while some Assyrians went to live in Israel and settled in Samaria. God had given Israel very strict directives pertaining to foreigners: *"You must not intermarry with them. Do not let your daughters and sons marry their sons and daughters, for they will lead your children away from me to worship other gods. Then the anger of the Lord will burn against you, and he will quickly destroy you"* (Deuteronomy 7:3-4). However, when the exiles returned, they disobeyed the Lord and intermarried with the foreigners, giving rise to a group of people who were part Jew and part Gentile living in the city of Samaria. The Jews despised those who lived in Samaria for intermarrying and serving pagan gods.

So this woman had difficulty understanding why this Jew was asking her for water. His reply confused her even more: *"If you only knew the gift God has for you and who you are speaking to, you would ask me, and I would give you living water"* (John 4:10). She asked, *"But sir, you don't have a rope or a bucket...and this well is very deep. Where would you get this living water?"* (verse 11)

Jesus took the opportunity to deliver His message. He offered her His spring of living water: *"Anyone who drinks this water will soon become thirsty again. But those who drink the water I give will never be thirsty again. It becomes a fresh, bubbling spring within them, giving them eternal life"* (verses 13-14). When she heard about the living water, she wanted to know more so that she could possess it. Jesus then asked her to get her husband and she said she didn't have one. Knowing the truth Jesus replied, *"You're right!*

You don't have a husband — for you have had five husbands, and you aren't even married to the man you're living with now. You certainly spoke the truth!" (verses 17-18).

Jesus gently exposed her lifestyle and her sin. His love for sinners does not eliminate the need to expose their sin. Jesus did not make a detour to take the time to minister to this woman, and then let her remain in her sin.

That is love in action. Your Love Walk will determine how you interact with those who need saving grace. Jesus gave an example of how to approach and interact with people who have no idea who He is. It started with an ordinary conversation about water, talking about natural water from the well. Then it shifted to Living Water. At first, she genuinely didn't understand; however, Jesus took the time to explain what He meant in a manner that became clear.

Although her sin was exposed, she didn't become defensive or argumentative; she continued talking to Jesus about worship. At the end of their discourse, she could see her condition for herself without pretence. Recognizing her sinfulness and her need for

God, she accepted Him as the Messiah. In fact, she became so excited that she left her water-pot at the well and ran to tell her whole village that Jesus was the Messiah. Change came into her life because she met Jesus and experienced the love of God.

Carrying our Burden through Love

Love makes demands on you. Jesus had to fulfill the demands of love in His life. He came to earth in response to God's love for man, and a desire to restore the fellowship that had been lost when man disobeyed God. His love cost something. When Jesus faced the burden of all our sins, He prayed, *"Father, if you are willing, please take this cup of suffering away from me. Yet I want your will to be done, not mine"* (Luke 22:42). He knew what He was about to face as the cup of suffering.

He took the burden of sin for the entire world when He died. God is holy and hates sin, but He loves the sinner. It's that love that drove Him to send His Son to redeem man from sin. The blood of animals was insufficient to redeem man from his sin, for redemption requires the blood of another human who is without sin. Unfortunately, with fallen man there is no one

witho...
man to ...

When the...
repaired the...
result of sin. H...
from Him. Whe...
sin of the world, H...
connection with His ...
agony, "'Eli, Eli, lema sa... *means 'My God, my God, why ha... ...oned me?'"* (Matthew 27:46). For the fi... ...ne the Son had lost communication with the Father. The Father and Son endured the pain of that momentary separation because of love for humanity.

Selfless Love

Coming back to 1 John 4:7-8, we see that John equated love with knowing God. If you love God, then as a child of God, you would imitate the behavior of your heavenly Father and walk in love. You may think that the task is beyond your ability. But remember, it's not you; it's the love of the Father working in and through you.

The world's system says that you love for the purpose of getting what you desire. So, if someone has something to offer, then it is

that relationship.
ve is not based on what

strate this, Jesus told a story about a
wish man on a journey, who was attacked
by robbers and left for dead. People from the
religious community walked by, took one look
at him and went on their way. Eventually, a
man from a different background came by and
had compassion on the man. He, too, was on a
journey. He was a Samaritan who cared for the
beaten man and took him to safety, and paid
someone to look after him. That was love in
action (Luke 10:30-36).

The people of His day knew that Jesus loved
them. He demonstrated that love when He took
the time to engage with and minister to them.
The Love Walk requires you to put people's
eternal well-being ahead of your personal
comfort or convenience. God is love.

Life Application

Have you failed in your attempt to show the
love of God to others? Has the hurt you have
experienced made you so bitter that the only

person you see is you? How has it impacted your life?

Ask God to restore His love for others in your heart. If you ask Him, He will do it.

Action Step

There are so many needy people in the world. Many times you don't see them because you are too busy. Slow down and develop a plan to show God's love to people in need.

Read and meditate on:

Deuteronomy 7:1-6; 10:17-19; Matthew 22:34-40; Luke 22:39-46; John 15:9-17,12; Acts 5:12-16; Romans 12:9-10; Ephesians 1:3-5; 1 Peter 1:18-22

The Word in My Life

I learned: _____

_____

Adjustments I can make: _____

_____

Prayer

Father, I have lost my first love. I have allowed people and things to rob me of my relationship with You. I want to love others the way You love me. Forgive me and restore to me the joy of my salvation, in Jesus' name, Amen.

Thought for the Day

Love is something I can do.

Two

LOVE IS KIND

Instead, be kind to each other, tenderhearted, forgiving one another, just as God through Christ has forgiven you.

(Ephesians 4:32)

Your walk with God should give rise to certain virtues in your life and kindness is one of them. The dictionary defines 'kindness' as 'doing something for someone and not expecting anything in return.' Kindness is respecting and helping others without waiting for someone to reciprocate. It implies that kindness does not look for a reward.

Kindness is more than being good to others; it involves showing sympathy and understanding. Many people come to know kindness through the actions of others who help them through their pain and discomfort. Some believe that kindness comes from people with high moral standards. However, the capacity to show kindness resides in every one of us.

Kindness Saved the Day

In Joshua chapter 2, Joshua dispatched two spies to gather information about Jericho. The men went into the city. Soon, it became common knowledge that there were strangers in their midst, which troubled the inhabitants of Jericho. The exploits of the children of Israel and their God were known to the surrounding nations and it generated fear. To preserve their safety, they felt it was necessary to find and kill the men.

These men found themselves in the house of Rahab, the harlot. Godly men were in a harlot's house, but she kept them safe. When the king of Jericho sent word to Rahab to disclose the location of the men, she replied that the men had come to her house but had since departed. Rahab had hidden the men on the roof to keep them safe. Women like Rahab lived on the city's wall, which ensured a steady stream of customers. Through those customers, she heard about what God was doing. Knowing that Jericho would fall, she risked her life to keep these men safe.

Rahab's actions ensured the success of the mission. The two men knew that without her help they would have lost their lives. The upright, upstanding citizens of Jericho decided that this was the only way to preserve their safety. Yet this morally bankrupt woman, Rahab the harlot found it in her heart to show kindness.

The foundation of true kindness is love. Love for God causes you to go the extra mile and give of yourself to others. Although, the definition of kindness says to expect nothing in return, sometimes you can reap the fruit of your kindness.

When it was time for the men to return to their camp, Rahab petitioned them, *"Now swear to me by the Lord that you will be kind to me and my family since I have helped you"* (verse 12). The men gave her a conditional response: she must not betray them and must safeguard their hideout. In return they promised to deliver her when Jericho fell.

The day came when Jericho fell. Joshua and his troops marched around the city for seven days in silence as the Lord commanded them. For the first six days they marched around the city once, and then returned to their camp. On the seventh day, they marched around the city seven times and, with a shout and the sound of the shofar, they saw the walls fall. God destroyed the city of Jericho but Rehab and her family were spared. Rahab reaped the fruit of her kindness.

Jesus took the time to show kindness to people He met. He did not allow the religious laws or cultural backgrounds to dictate how to interact with others. There are so many norms that dictate how people interact especially when there is an individual that is not accepted by the group. Godly people who believe someone has violated their godly principles for living can become a mob.

Kindness Supersedes the Law

One day while Jesus was teaching in the temple, the religious leaders brought a woman before Him. She was caught in the act of adultery, so the religious leaders pointed out that her sentence was death. The Law of Moses says,

"If a man is discovered committing adultery, both he and the woman must die. In this way, you will purge Israel of such evil" (Deuteronomy 22:22). The law clearly states that both parties must die for breaking the law and the religious leaders felt justified in trying to enforce it.

When you are in a crowd, it's easy for emotion to influence your thinking. Partial truth can be damaging. Yes, she was involved in an adulterous relationship but she could not have committed adultery alone. They left the man but brought the woman before Jesus. You can acknowledge that her actions were sinful, but, if they chose to hold only one party accountable for the actions of two, then they were breaking the very law they were trying to uphold.

They had no problem allowing the man to escape the sentence. Could it be he was a friend or someone of high office? The woman was not considered someone of value, so they paraded her through the streets, humiliating her and then brought her to Jesus to validate their righteous conduct. Jesus didn't give them the response they expected. They thought they had Him boxed in a religious dilemma: whichever way He responded, they would be able to discredit Him.

Jesus didn't look up at them, but used His fingers to write in the sand. Although they kept demanding a response, He did not reply. Eventually, He gave his response, *"All right, but let the one who has never sinned throw the first stone!"* (John 8:7). They were so busy condemning the woman and her sinful life; they forgot that they were just as guilty before God as the woman caught in the act of adultery. They were unable to proceed with the execution because Jesus turned the tables on them. After a while, everyone left except Jesus and the woman.

"Where are your accusers? Didn't even one of them condemn you?" He asked her.

When she said no, He responded, *"Neither do I. Go and sin no more."*

In life, there will always be people who come up short who don't fit in, people who are different. That does not give anyone the right to treat them differently. So the way you respond to others and their circumstances will determine the condition of your Love Walk. The crowd was not walking in love. In his letter Peter says,

"Most important of all, continue to show deep love for each other, for love covers a multitude of sins" (1 Peter 4:8). That is what Jesus did. He covered the woman but did not condone her behavior. He told her to change her lifestyle and live right before God.

You don't need a platform to be kind. In whatever state you are in, the capacity to show kindness dwells in you. The homeless man can show kindness in his community because he can share his supplies with someone who has nothing at all. The child on the playground can choose not to join in when the group wants to bully another student because they look different. The office worker can offer a helping hand to the new employee struggling to complete a task. In every human being is the capacity to show kindness.

When the spies went out, they had no idea what was before them. They never thought that their lives would be connected to a woman of ill repute. Yet, her kindness made the difference in their lives and their mission. As a result, their kindness made the difference in her life and that of her family. That's the power of your

Love Walk; it makes the difference in the lives of those you meet.

Matthew 7:12 says, *"Do to others whatever you would like them to do to you. This is the essence of all that is taught in the law and the prophets."* While the world tells you not to expect anything in return, God says kindness will find its way back to you. Love is kind.

Life Application

Do you have a challenge showing kindness to some people? Why? What are some things you can do to bring change in your life?

Action Step

There are many opportunities to show kindness. When the opportunity arises, put aside your feelings and allow the love of God to shine through you. What are some things you can do to show kindness?

Read and meditate on:

Genesis 24:12-27; Exodus 1:15-21; Joshua 2; Ruth 2:20-21; 2 Samuel 9; John 8:1-11; Acts:16:25-33; 28:1-2; Titus 3:4-7; 2 Peter 1:5-7

The Word in My Life

I learned: _____

_____

Adjustments I can make: _____

_____

Prayer

Father, I want to love by showing kindness. Sometimes I neglect to use the opportunities that would demonstrate my Love Walk. Forgive me and help me to express Your love for others by showing kindness, in Jesus' name. Amen.

Thought for the Day

An act of kindness goes a long way.

$\mathcal{T}hree$

LOVE FORGIVES OTHERS

Make allowance for each other's faults, and forgive anyone who offends you. Remember, the Lord forgave you, so you must forgive others.

(Colossians 3:13)

It is easy to associate love with forgiveness. In the context of a loving relationship, it's so much easier to forgive. Parents love their children, so it's not difficult for a parent to forgive a child. Yet in our society, it's not uncommon for people to hold grudges, sometimes for years. It's easier to hold on to that feeling of resentment than to let go. It's rare for an issue to exist when only one participant is at fault. But if you belong to a group or organization you are likely to offend someone. It's not the intent, but it happens. This is not an isolated occurrence; it happens continuously where people gather. When offense happens, there must be resolution to preserve the community. Resolution comes through forgiveness.

So what is forgiveness? The dictionary gives a variety of definitions. 'To forgive' is 'to cease to feel anger and resentment against an offender.' It's letting go of past grudges or lingering anger against a person. Forgiveness is letting go of your desire for justice. Forgiveness wipes the slate clean. Forgiveness is like walking uphill on a hot day.

With a definition that extensive, forgiveness is not an easy task. Wounded people hurt and their pain is real. So many times there is a rush to fix the situation without acknowledging the pain the individual experienced. It's important to remember that, even though you don't believe that those words or actions could cause pain; if the individual experienced pain, then their pain is real.

The above verse states that there should be some measure of allowance for the faults of others. This is not an excuse for bad behavior;

however, it does mean that you need to give others some leeway because at some point in your life, you would need some measure of allowance yourself.

The Price of Unforgiveness

To teach on forgiveness, Jesus told a parable in Matthew 18. A certain man owed a sizable amount of money but was unable to pay his creditor. The custom was to sell the man, his wife, his children and all his possessions to pay off his debt. This man fell to the ground and begged his creditor for mercy. His creditor had compassion on him and forgave his debt. He made allowance for his debt.

Well, that same man, who had experienced the compassion of his creditor, met someone who owed him a small amount of money. He did not make an allowance for this man even though the man pleaded with him. This wicked man sent his debtor to prison until he could pay off his debt.

When his colleagues saw what transpired, they reported the incident to the wicked man's creditor. His creditor responded, "*You evil servant! I forgave you that tremendous debt because you pleaded with me. Shouldn't you have mercy on your fellow servant, just as I had mercy on you?' Then the angry king sent the man to prison to be tortured until he had paid his entire debt"* (Matthew 18:32-34).

You might wonder what generated such an unmerciful response in this individual. Many times that is the way many people react to offences. But the bottom line is you have to forgive so that you can be forgiven. As you mature in Christ, it becomes easier to say, "I'm sorry" just as we pray to God to *"forgive us our sins, as we have forgiven those who sin against us"* (Matthew 6:12).

What happens after you say you're sorry? Some people cannot move on from there. When the wound of betrayal is inflicted by the hand of someone close, many times it's not so easy to move forward. People of faith believe that forgiveness happens instantly. In some instances it can but in many cases it takes time. No situation is the same. But, whether it happens over time or immediately, it must happen.

How many times should we forgive the same person for the same offence? Let's see what Jesus said. *"Then Peter came to him and asked,*

'Lord, how often should I forgive someone who sins against me? Seven times?' 'No, not seven times,' Jesus replied, *'but seventy times seven!'"* (Matthew 18:21-22) Does it mean that you have to get out a note book and keep track so you will know when you get to seventy times seven plus one? No, it means you need to develop a lifestyle of forgiveness.

Developing a lifestyle of forgiveness is challenging but it is not impossible. First, forgiveness is a choice you make in your head not your heart. You will forgive. The man in the parable chose to treat his colleague harshly after he experienced forgiveness from his master. Therefore, forgiveness is what you choose to do or not do.

David Makes Allowance

There are some powerful examples of forgiveness in the Bible. When David first met King Saul, Goliath was on the battlefield taunting Israel day and night for forty days. The children of Israel were living in fear of the giant. But the Spirit of the Lord was upon David and he slew Goliath. While Israel celebrated David's victory, Saul viewed him as a threat to his kingdom. So he pursued David to kill him. One day, David and his men had the opportunity to kill Saul. But David extended forgiveness to Saul. *"So David restrained his men and did not let them kill Saul"* (1 Samuel 24:7). Saul never knew how close he had come to losing his life. Many would have looked the other way and allowed the men to exact revenge, but David made allowance for Saul.

Unfortunately, society has become an arena of selfishness. Individuals are more concerned about the way issues and circumstances affect their lives. Even when we have received forgiveness, we still find it difficult to go out and forgive one another. The enemy of the soul of man is cunning and crafty. He knows that an unforgiving spirit will erode our relationship with God.

God placed the bar of forgiveness very high. *If you forgive those who sin against you, your heavenly Father will forgive you. But if you refuse to forgive others, your Father will not forgive your sins"* (Matthew 6:14-15). It may not be what you want to do but it is something you have to do.

So let's work on forgiveness. Remember, when you withhold forgiveness for others, God will withhold forgiveness for you. It's impossible to love without forgiving. Love forgives others.

Life Application

Is there a situation that is difficult for you to forget because the pain runs deep? How does it make you feel?

Action Step

Take some time and reflect on God. He is Love. God put His love in action when Jesus came and died for the sins of the world. What are some things you can do to make allowance for those who hurt you so you can forgive them?

Read and meditate on:

Genesis 33:1-16; 1 Samuel 24:2; Samuel 19:19-23; Proverbs 17:9; Matthew 6:7-15; 18:21-35; Mark 11:22-25; Luke 17:3-4; Hebrews 10:15-18

The Word in My Life

I learned: _____

_____

Adjustments I can make: _____

_____

Prayer

Father, forgive me for refusing to make allowances for those that hurt me. At times I focus on what they did instead of what I need to do. I want to let go of my desire for justice. Help me to let go of my unforgiveness, so that You can forgive me, in Jesus' name, Amen.

Thought for the Day

I will forgive so that I can be forgiven.

Four

LOVE DOES NOT JUDGE

"Do not judge others, and you will not be judged. For you will be treated as you treat others. The standard you use in judging is the standard by which you will be judged."

(Matthew 7:1-2)

We tend to make judgments all the time. You walk down the street, and you see someone homeless and you judge. "That person is lazy and does not want to work or is an addict," you think. That can be the true for some, but not necessarily for everyone who lives on the street. You have no way to determine if what you believe is true. You just judged that person.

That does not say that you should walk into any environment and let your guard down. There is a difference between being judgmental and cautious. Judgmental eyes can look down on others, while the eyes of caution promote self preservation. Jesus taught His followers to be very careful when they look at others because each person creates their own standards of evaluation based on the way they judge others.

Paul gives this same caution, *"So don't make judgments about anyone ahead of time — before the Lord returns. For he will bring our darkest secrets to light and will reveal our private motives. Then God will give to each one whatever praise is due"* (1 Corinthians 4:5). When you are quick to judge, you are quick to condemn. You have no idea if the standard of judgment you are using is valid.

In our justice system there is a process when a person is suspected of committing a crime. The individual is always presumed innocent until proven guilty. It is up to the prosecution to provide evidence to convince the jury that the individual did indeed commit the crime. The defense presumes innocence and presents evidence to disprove the presumption of guilt. The judge presides over the case and ensures that everyone operates within the boundaries of the law.

However, the evidence at times can be misleading if you have limited information. When you look at Job, you don't know what to think. When you meet him in chapter 1, he is a good man. This man was so committed to living right before God that he even offered sacrifices to God in case his children sinned while they were socializing.

How Job's Friends Got It All Wrong

In fact, God endorsed Job. He said, *"He is the finest man in all the earth. He is blameless — a man of complete integrity. He fears God and stays away from evil"* (Job 1:8). That should have indicated an even and smooth path for Job. It didn't! When God endorsed Job, He was speaking to the enemy. He was boasting about Job the way a father boasts about his son.

The enemy didn't agree with that statement. He had his own ideas about Job's integrity. He said that Job was being faithful to God for the sake of benefits but that Job's attitude would change if his circumstances did. So God allowed the enemy to change Job's circumstances. One day, while Job was going about his daily activities, a messenger ran towards him and told Job that as a result of a raid his animals were stolen, his employees were killed and he alone survived the attack. While he was speaking another messenger arrived with more bad news: all his sheep and shepherds were gone but he escaped. While he was speaking, another messenger reported that his camels were stolen and his servants killed. Finally, another messenger arrived to report that all his children had been killed when a great wind struck the house down (Job 1:13-19).

This was a defining moment for Job. His response would determine his future. God was confident of Job's integrity and Job came through. Job did not blame God for his misfortunes. Instead, he said *"I came naked from my mother's womb and I will be naked when I leave. The Lord gave me what I had, and the Lord has taken it away. Praise the name of the Lord! In all of this, Job did not sin by blaming God"* (Job 1:19). Job worshipped God in the midst of the biggest calamity of his life.

When his plan failed, the enemy went before God to further accuse Job. Now this time he believed that Job cared more about his life and health than his possessions. God allowed the enemy to touch Job's body. *"So Satan left the Lord's presence, and he struck Job with terrible boils from head to foot"* (Job 2:7). Job was sitting in the ashes, scraping the boils on his body, when his friends visited. When they saw his condition, they were heartbroken. But, as time went by, their attitude towards Job changed.

As they continued to evaluate Job's life, they looked at the evidence and judged Job. He had lost his possessions and family. They reasoned that God did not allow this calamity in Job's life by accident. There must be some underlying conditions or secret sin in his life; his predicament was nothing else but God's judgment.

The problem with judging others is that it changes your attitude towards them. When Job's friends first saw him, they could hardly recognize him because of his affliction. His grief touched their hearts. Following the custom of the day, they tore their clothes and threw dust in the air over their heads. *"Then they sat on the ground with him for seven days and nights. No one said a word to Job, for they saw that his suffering was too great for words"* (Job 2:13). Job's burdens felt lighter as his friends supported him.

However, very soon these men took it upon themselves to show Job the error of his ways. They took turns telling Job that there was sin in his life. The first friend to speak, Eliphaz said, *"My experience shows that those who plant trouble and cultivate evil will harvest the same"* (Job 4:8). The second friend Bildad spoke, *"Does God twist justice? Does the Almighty twist what is right? Your children must have sinned against him, so their punishment was well deserved"* (Job 8:3-4). The third friend Zophar warned, *"Listen! God is doubtless punishing you far less than you deserve!"* (Job 11:6). These friends sincerely believed that they were speaking the truth to Job in his distress.

Before anyone stands to judge another, that individual must be mindful that the process will also reveal the rubric for his own evaluation. If you are harsh with others, your own judgment for wrongdoing will be harsh. It's premature to draw a conclusion when you don't have all the information. *"God alone, who gave the law, is the Judge. He alone has the power to save or to destroy. So what right do you have to judge your neighbor?"* (James 4:12) It is worth remembering that God is the only one with all the facts. Moreover, He is also the only one who has the integrity and moral character to judge fairly. Instead, exercise caution. *"There will be no mercy for those who have not shown mercy to others. But if you have been merciful, God will be merciful when he judges you"* (James 2:13).

In the end, God reprimanded Job's friends. They had to go and apologize to him and ask him to pray for them. *"When Job prayed for his friends, the* LORD *restored his fortunes. In fact, the* LORD *gave him twice as much as before!"* (Job 10:42)

It's easy to judge another. But when you are on a Love Walk, you have to resist the urge to judge. Change your narrative and say like Isaiah did, *"Be strong, and do not fear, for your God is coming to destroy your enemies. He is coming to save you"* (Isaiah 35:4). It's so easy to be the voice of gloom and doom. Make a change and encourage someone in distress. And when you are tempted to judge others, don't. Love does not judge.

Life Application

Do you have a tendency to form opinions before you have all the information? What problems can you see when you are quick to judge others?

Action Step

The next time you receive some information about something or someone, remind yourself that you don't know the whole story, and refuse to form an opinion. What are some things you can do to help change the way you judge others?

Read and mediate on:

Job 1:6-22; 2:1-13; 4:1-8; 8:1-4; 11:1-6; Matthew 5:3-12; Luke 6:37-42; 1 Corinthians 4:5-7; James 2:1-13; 4:11-12

The Word in my Life

I learned: _____

_____

Adjustments I can make: _____

_____

Prayer

Father, I have been guilty of judging others. Many times I formed opinions and judged others unfairly. I am aware that You will judge me the way I judge others. Help me to always see the best in the people I meet, in Jesus' name, Amen.

Thought for the Day

When I judge others, I myself will be judged.

Five

LOVE LIVES IN FELLOWSHIP

But if we are living in the light, as God is in the light, then we have fellowship with each other, and the blood of Jesus, his Son, cleanses us from all sin.

(1 John 1:7)

Whenever people think of fellowship, they usually think of social events. Of course fellowship occurs when you interact with others, but it goes deeper than mere social gatherings. The dictionary defines 'fellowship' as a 'friendly association, especially with people who share the same interests.' But Christian fellowship is so much more. It revolves around the Father, the Son and the Holy Spirit. As 1 John 1:4 says, *"We are writing these things so that you may fully share our joy."* That joy is in fellowship through God: that is the connection. So your fellowship needs to be plugged in to the same connection because the spiritual precedes the social in fellowship.

Love is the source of authentic fellowship and without genuine love, authentic fellowship does not exist. The world will judge your God by your love. They will look at your Love Walk. Your Love Walk determines and directs your actions. *"So we are lying if we say we have fellowship with God but go on living in spiritual darkness; we are not practicing the truth"* (1 John 1:6).

Unity in the Midst of Diversity

The church in the book of Acts expressed that love and fellowship in a manner that proved to the world that the followers of Jesus were indeed children of God. They formed a community grounded in love where everything was shared. There was no distinction between those who had much and those who had little. These differences were lost when they sold their possessions and gave to those in need.

The world was looking at these believers as they went to the Temple together, ate meals together, had fun and fellowship together. Their Love Walk was so strong that people wanted to join them. They saw how that love united them. As a result, this small diverse group could evangelize their world. The gospel penetrated the hearts of men and women because of their Love Walk.

So how did it all begin? The early church began in Acts chapter 2. In the midst of a religious gathering, there was confusion because the Holy Spirit had just fallen on the disciples and the community wanted clarity. Peter got up and preached the first gospel message. The message was so stirring that they baptized about three thousand people that day and continued to baptize people on a daily basis. These believers, as they were called, formed a community that spent time together, were taught together, ate together and prayed together.

John experienced the power of the Love Walk. He remembered how they impacted their community with the quality of their fellowship. Yes, there were disagreements because people are different and those differences could take the form of disagreements. Discord is always lurking when people gather, even in the house of God. But your Love Walk will determine how you manage discord.

In Galatians Chapter 2, there was a serious altercation between Peter and Paul. Peter had open fellowship with the Gentile Christians at Antioch. However, when some of his Jewish brothers arrived, he disassociated himself from the believers there. Because he was a leader, others followed Peter's duplicity, which is, behaving one way with Jews and another with Gentiles. To set things in order, Paul confronted him publicly because he wanted to protect authentic Christian fellowship. It was not Paul's intension to embarrass Peter in front of everyone.

Peter responded with grace. He listened to and acknowledged that his actions were inconsistent with his Love Walk. I believed that Peter valued Paul for his honesty and commitment to the work of the Lord. When Peter wrote 2 Peter 3, he referred to Paul as, "our beloved brother," and commented on the wisdom that Paul received from God. This shows that their disagreement did not disrupt their Love Walk.

In a world filled with discord, how can individuals resolve conflicts peacefully? The first thing that is necessary to resolve conflict in a community is a desire to make things right in accordance with the will of God. That desire must exist in all the participants. Each person needs to see the benefit for themselves and the group to resolve the conflict.

Resolving conflicts in the community requires the same level of accountability from each member. In some communities, status and prestige influence the engagement process, creating inequality in the hierarchy of authority. This inequality gives rise to a class structure creating an imbalance which makes the resolution elusive.

Early intervention is necessary in these conflicts because the members are motivated to find common ground. The longer the spirit of discord resides in the community, the more difficult it becomes to regain control. When the conflict gets to this point, the enemy is in total control. When this happens in the community of faith, only the Holy Spirit can bring about change.

John 10:10 says, *"The thief's purpose is to steal and kill and destroy. My purpose is to give them a rich and satisfying life."* The thief wants to destroy the fellowship and put a limp in your Love Walk. Then, when the fellowship is destroyed, he points an accusing finger. This is the time to go to God and pray Psalm 139:23-24 over your life: *"Search me, O God, and know my heart; test me and know my anxious thoughts. Point out anything in me that offends you, and lead me along the path of everlasting life."*

Prior to this, the problem was a simple conflict; now it's escalated into a problem of the heart. Only God can bring healing at this time. When you consider the issue between Peter and Paul, you realize that they never let the matter become a heart problem. Paul saw a problem that needed intervention and so he intervened. Peter saw how his actions were destroying his Love Walk, and he made the necessary adjustments.

There is healing for every problem and situation that people encounter, including problems with fellowship. The early church evangelized their world because they had things in common, and that made their bond strong. The enemy works overtime to sow seeds of discord because he understands the power in unity. But when we walk in agreement, nothing can break that bond, for Jesus is in our midst. *"For where two or three gather together as my followers, I am there among them"* (Matthew 18:20).

Jesus Christ comes in and fellowships when His children gather in His name. Then amazing things begin to happen. *"The members of the council were amazed when they saw the boldness of Peter and John, for they could see that they were ordinary men with no special training in the Scriptures. They also recognized them as men who had been with Jesus"* (Acts 4:13). When you fellowship with Jesus, people recognize you are special.

The enemy will do everything in his power to destroy the fellowship of the believers. He knows that if he can cause turmoil, it would impact your Love Walk. When the community of faith comes together and works in fellowship, there is no limit to what they can do. Matthew 18:19 says, *"If two of you agree here on earth concerning anything you ask, my Father in heaven will do it for you."* So let's agree to walk together in the bond of unity. Love thrives in fellowship.

Life Application

Have you been struggling with authentic fellowship? What have you done to correct the problem? Did it work? Lack of authentic fellowship affects your Love Walk.

Action Step

Take some time and read 1 John 1. Acknowledge that you are not practicing the truth. What are some things you can do to strengthen your Love Walk?

Read and mediate on:

Proverbs 27:17; Matthew 8:15-20; John 10:1-15; Acts 2:42-47; 4:13-22; Romans 1:12-17; 1 Corinthians 1:10:10-17; Galatians 2:11-21; Ephesians 4:2-6; 2 Peter 3:14; 1 John 1:1-10

The Word in My Life

I learned: _____

_____

Adjustments I can make: _____

_____

Prayer

Father, I acknowledge that I have not been walking in love. There is discord in my life that is affecting my Love Walk. I want to live in the light as You are in the light. Help me to mend broken fellowship, so I can strengthen my Love Walk, in Jesus' name, Amen.

Thought for the Day

I can overcome discord with love.

Six

LOVE IS OBEDIENT

Jesus replied, "All who love me will do what I say. My Father will love them, and we will come and make our home with each of them."

(John 14:23).

*I*t's inconceivable to do what's right without loving God. Doing right involves the heart. It's more than just knowing the right thing to do in any given situation. It's doing what's right in God's eyes, not what's acceptable to society. Loving God leads you to obedience.

Your Love Walk will determine how obedient you are. Obedience is easy when everything is going the way you like it, when the crowd is in agreement with what you are doing. What do you do when you have to stand alone because your position is not popular? Your Love Walk will direct your action.

The Great Escape

Jonah, a man in the Old Testament, found himself in a tight situation. God had given him the directive to go on a mission to Nineveh but Jonah decided to go in the opposite direction from God's destination. Some assignments can be difficult and you want to run away. But love compels you to obey. However, Jonah's solution expressed the condition of his Love Walk. He was so determined to do things his way that he paid the fare and got on a ship bound for Tarshish.

Jonah disobeyed the instructions from God. He allowed his personal feelings to get in the way because he didn't like the people of Nineveh and he was not going there. But in John 14:23 Jesus stated that all who love Him will do what He says. Everyone, at one time or another, has behaved like Jonah. You can generate a list of reasons to turn away from obeying God: you want to fit in with a particular group; you want to belong. So, although you know God is looking for obedience, you ignore it.

It is your love for God that constrains you to obey; that love will drive you to do what is pleasing to Him. In other words, love is obedient. Jonah discovered something about disobeying God when He sends you on a mission. He ran from God but he couldn't hide from Him. You see, while that ship was at sea, a storm arose. The crew tried everything they could to prevent the destruction of the ship. During all this commotion, Jonah was asleep.

The captain woke him up and asked him to pray to his God. After casting lots, they determined that it was Jonah who was the cause of the storm and threw him overboard. Being thrown overboard must have been the most frightening experience of his life because the storm was raging. *"I sank beneath the waves, and the waters closed over me. Seaweed wrapped itself around my head"* (Jonah 2:5). He saw the end of his life; and at that time he prayed. He called on God from the land of the dead (Jonah 2:2).

Jonah was then swallowed by a huge fish and spent three days and three nights in its belly. I know it would certainly not be a pleasant experience especially when big animals eat smaller animals for food. There could have been some live fish in the belly as well as dead animals. The stench must have been unbearable. It was a dark and lonely place. It was the place of disobedience. It's possible to derail your Love Walk with disobedience. But God in His mercy gave him a second chance. The fish delivered Jonah to Nineveh. That set him on course to accomplish his mission.

This time Jonah didn't try to run away. He went and did what God instructed him to do. Obedience requires you to submit to God's plan. Your priority becomes what pleases God as opposed to what pleases you. When, like Jonah, your focus becomes your desire and not what God directs you to do, then you are walking in disobedience and sooner or later will suffer the consequences.

Mocked for Obedience

In contrast, Noah had a different response when God spoke to him. God didn't give Noah an easy task to go and tell people to repent. Noah had to build a huge boat. Man had become corrupt and the wickedness was so great that God was sorry that He had made man. *"But Noah found favor with the LORD"* (Genesis 6:8) because he walked uprightly before God. So God decided that He would destroy the earth with water but He would preserve Noah, his family and the male and female pair of each animal species.

Noah started to build the boat. It must have been a difficult task. Scholars can't agree as to how long it took to build the ark but it was a very long time. One can only imagine the ridicule and humiliation that Noah endured in a region that experienced little rain. He was the butt of jokes in his community. But, despite all that he had to endure, he remained faithful to the task. *"So Noah did everything exactly as God had commanded him"* (Genesis 6:22). Then one day God shut the doors of the ark and the flood came.

Sometimes walking in obedience to God is not popular. But God rewards all those who obey. Look what Jesus says to His disciples: *"All who love me will do what I say. My Father will love them, and we will come and make our home with each of them"* (John 14:23). If there was nothing else, that would be enough. For those who want to live forever, you have only to obey Jesus, *"I tell you the truth, anyone who obeys my teaching will never die!"* (John 8:51). God will also bless you while you are walking in obedience. *"If you listen to these commands of the Lord your God* that I am giving you today, and if you carefully obey them, the LORD will make you the head and not the tail, and you will always be on top and never at the bottom" (Deuteronomy 28:13).

God places a high value on obedience. Jesus Christ was the perfect example of obedience. He had to lay aside His heavenly splendor and come to earth and live in human form, for no other reason but to become the sacrifice for mankind. *"He humbled himself in obedience to God and died a criminal's death on a cross"* (Philippians 2:8). He understood what was needed and the price He had to pay. Jesus Christ, who was God in human form, was obedient to the Father.

Love is obedient. When you walk in disobedience, you are not walking in love. Jonah was able with God's help to correct his error. How much easier it would have been for him to obey the first time! God does not fellowship with disobedience. If you want to maintain your relationship with God, you have to obey. Love is obedient.

Life Application
Are you having difficulty obeying God's Word? What are some things that stand in your way?

Determine what changes you need to make and list them.

Action Step

In your heart you want to engage in a Love Walk that shows that you walk in obedience to God. What are some things you would like to implement in your life to enhance your Love Walk?

Read and meditate on:

Genesis 6:1-8; Deuteronomy 5:32-33; 28:1-14; 1 Peter 1:8; 1 John 5:3; Jonah 1:1-3; 2;1-10; John 14:23-24; Acts 26:12-20; Philippians 2:5-11

The Word in My Life

I learned: _____

_____

Adjustments I can make: _____

_____

Prayer

Father, I am having difficulty obeying You. Obedience is important in my Love Walk. I want to live in obedience to Your word. Help me in my struggle to walk right before You, in Jesus' name, Amen.

Thought for the Day

God desires obedience.

$\mathcal{S}even$

LOVE DRIVES OUT FEAR

Such love has no fear, because perfect love expels all fear. If we are afraid, it is for fear of punishment, and this shows that we have not fully experienced his perfect love.

(1 John 4:18)

Fear! It's not a word many people love to use when they describe themselves. Men will do everything they can to conceal the fact that fear is lurking in their minds because society has conditioned men to believe that real men are fearless. So men have to live up to this image that they cannot show fear in any situation because fear is not manly.

Women, on the other hand, are expected to exhibit fear. Fearlessness and femininity cannot coexist in our society – at least that's the belief in some circles. However, many women neutralize situations that evoke fear of physical attack with defense training to help them feel more confident in protecting themselves.

Whatever is the case; fear is a part of life and is a necessary component for your protection and wellbeing. If you are crossing the street and you look up and see a car speeding towards you, you will run to safety. That is the self-preservation kind of fear working to protect you and keep you safe. However, there is a fear that is paralyzing and seeks to control and dominate your life so that you are unable to function adequately. That fear is not from God.

The world has a name for this paralyzing fear: phobia. Phobia manifests itself in anxiety of such magnitude that it prohibits the individuals from enjoying their lives. The origin of this fear had nothing to do with tangible things, but it ignites an emotional response which is real for the person with the phobia. As a result, that person will refrain from the activity that triggers the fear. Most of us are familiar with claustrophobia, the fear of closed-in spaces.

In the same way that phobia impacts your natural life; fear can paralyze your spiritual life. Paul, who mentored Timothy as his spiritual son, was aware there were many hardships in ministry that had the potential to make them fearful. So Paul tells him, *"For God has not given us a spirit of fear and timidity, but of power, love, and self-discipline"* (2 Timothy 1:7). Yes, Paul knew that some experiences in life could undermine the power of God in his life if he were to give in to fear.

Judgment on Belshazzar

There are those who walk in fear because they are guilty of wrongdoing. In Daniel chapter 5, Belshazzar, the Babylonian king hosted a huge social gathering. During the festivities, he requested the gold and silver cups that his father Nebuchadnezzar had removed from the temple in Jerusalem to be brought out. He used these holy vessels to drink wine and praise their pagan gods. While they were eating and drinking, a finger from a man's hand wrote a message in a foreign language on the wall. It was so chilling that *"His face turned pale with fright. His knees knocked together in fear and his legs gave way beneath him"* (Daniel 5:6). Belshazzar knew that he had violated the holy vessels of God and was terrified.

Belshazzar called all the learned men to decipher what the note said but they were unable to find the meaning of the message. Then the queen mother told him about Daniel and the gifting in his life, confident that Daniel would be able to decode the writing. The king sent for Daniel and promised him position and wealth but Daniel refused these things; however, he did explain the writing. God was about to punish Belshazzar. He reminded him about the experiences of his father, Nebuchadnezzar and the judgment of God on his life. And God judged Belshazzar. His days as ruler came to an end that very night when the Medo-Persian army invaded the city and he was killed.

Gideon's Doubts

Then there are those who are afraid because they feel totally helpless in bringing about change in their situation: like Gideon in the Book of Judges. The Book of Judges chronicles the history of the Jews when they came to the Promised Land. Moses was dead and Joshua was about to die but, unlike Moses, Joshua had not groomed a leader to lead the people.

However, the people had promised Joshua that they would walk right before God; but after his death, they turned to their own ways, *"In those days Israel had no king; all the people did whatever seemed right in their own eyes"*(Judges 17:6). The people had a history of going through cycles of repentance and turning back to idols. *"This made the* Lord burn with anger against Israel, so he handed them over to raiders who stole their possessions. He turned them over to their enemies all around, and they were no longer able to resist them"* (Judges 2:14).

Whenever their enemies subdued them, they called on the Lord for deliverance, and God raised up Judges to deliver them. On one occasion the children of Israel cried out to the Lord because the oppression by the Midianites was so great. Whenever the planted crops and were about to harvest them, their enemies would destroy the crops leaving them with no food. God sent the angel of the Lord to appoint the next judge, Gideon. Gideon was so afraid of the Midianites that he was threshing his wheat in a winepress. But the angel of the Lord addressed Gideon, *"Mighty hero, the* LORD is with you!"* (Judges 6:12) Mighty was the last thing Gideon felt, so great was his fear.

The angel didn't recount the wrongdoings of the people that brought their enemies upon them; instead he directed him to the solution. So God set Gideon as a judge to deliver Israel from the hands of the Midianites. *"Go with the strength you have, and rescue Israel from the Midianites. I am sending you!"* said the angel to Gideon (Judges 6:14) and God gave Gideon divine directions and assurance.

Gideon was so conditioned to living in fear of the Midianites that he had difficulty trusting God. Gideon harbored some doubt that the Lord was with them. He looked at their circumstances and felt that God had abandoned them. Fear is a foe and if you cuddle your fear you will not be able to accomplish anything. In fact, Gideon listed all the requirements that disqualified him from the leadership role that God now called him into. His family was not prominent among the tribes and he was the least in his family. Now fear's cousin, low self esteem, was having a party in Gideon's head. He had difficulty getting past the fear even though the angel reassured him. *"The Lord said to him, "I will be with you. And you will destroy the Midianites as if you were fighting against one man"* (Judges 6:16).

When you walk in fear, it's not easy to lay aside that fear to receive what God has designed for your life. Gideon continued to express his doubts and fears but God patiently ministered to him until he was able to step out in faith. His first task was to destroy the altar of Baal. He couldn't do it during the day, but he did it at night – afraid. He did not let that fear prevent him from obeying God.

There is not one person alive who has not experienced fear. Gideon was afraid but he spent some time with the angel of the Lord and in the process, faced his fear. What can you do when you are afraid to take a step God has designed for you? God is aware of the fear that controls you and He is willing to give you the power to work through your fear. When you walk in God's love, you show that you are willing to trust Him in your Love Walk. There will always be circumstances that bring fear into your life. You can choose to allow fear to keep you in its grip, or you can choose to trust God. When you love God, your Love Walk will not be controlled by fear because perfect love expels all fear (1 John 4:18). Love drives out fear.

Life Application

How do you respond when fear comes in like a river and wants to overwhelm you? Do you face your challenge like a champion? What can you do?

Action Step

Take some time and search the Word of God and for scriptures about fear. What does the Bible say? Meditate on these scriptures and speak them over your life. List two things you can do differently the next time fear wants to control your life.

Read and meditate on:

Exodus 3:1-6; Numbers 13:25-33; Judges 6:6-16; Isaiah 41:8-10; Daniel 5:1-6; Matthew 6:25-34; John 14:27-31; Philippians 4:6-7; I Peter 5:6-7

The Word in My Life

I learned: _____

_____

Adjustments I can make: _____

_____

Prayer

Father, I thank You for Your word in my life. I know in the past I have allowed fear to control me. I want change to come into my life. Help me to remember that You are with me, so I don't need to be afraid, in Jesus' name, Amen.

Thought for the Day

I will fear no evil.

Eight

LOVE DOES WHAT IS RIGHT

Remember, it is sin to know what you ought to do and then not do it.

(James 4:17)

The Love Walk takes backbone. At times it's difficult to live the walk. There are times most people would wish for the opportunity to live their life as they please. The Love Walk does not offer that opportunity. Most people understand that not obeying the command to love one another is sin. *"It's a sin to despise one who is less fortunate than you, but when you are kind to the poor, you will prosper and be blessed"* (Proverbs 14:21 TPT). Just about everyone has met or knows someone who needs help. While it is impossible to help every person in need who crosses your path, there is at least one person that you can help.

Jesus lived His life reaching out and helping people from all walks of life. He did not discriminate. He modeled doing what was right. He wanted His followers to understand the importance of showing love by doing what is right, so He shared these words with them, *"But anyone who hears my teaching and doesn't obey it is foolish, like a person who builds a house on sand"* (Matthew 7:26).

It is the same with the foundation of a house. A strong foundation is necessary to withstand the weight of the structure. When you think of sand, you think of loose, grainy soil, something that has difficulty holding its shape. So, if your foundation is built on sand, as the earth shifts and moves, so will the foundation. Jesus went on to say, *"When the rains and floods come and the winds beat against that house, it will collapse with a mighty crash"* (Matthew 7:27).

Investing for Profit

So if you neglect to do what is right when you know it is right, that neglect is sin. The question is: how do you know? Jesus told a parable to illustrate that neglecting to do what is right has consequences. In Matthew 25, an employer decided to take a trip. He entrusted his employees with bags of silver. One man had five bags, another two and the last man had one. The individual with five bags invested the five bags and earned another five bags of interest. The second man with two bags doubled his investment, so now he had four. However, the third man with one bag decided that it was too much work to invest the money, so he took the bag of silver and buried it in the ground.

When the master returned, it was time to account for the money. When the first two men presented the earnings on their investment to the master, he was delighted and made plans to celebrate.

Now, it was time for the third man to account for his activities. He responded, *"Master, I knew you were a harsh man, harvesting crops you didn't plant and gathering crops you didn't cultivate. I was afraid I would lose your money, so I hid it in the earth. Look, here is your money back"* (Matthew 25:24-25). The employer became angry and reprimanded the man, *"You wicked and lazy servant! If you knew I harvested crops I didn't plant and gathered crops I didn't cultivate, why didn't you deposit my money in the bank? At least I could have gotten some interest on it"* (Matthew 25:26-27).

Clearly, this employee was derelict in his duties. He knew that the bank would give him some interest on the deposit but neglected to do it. He willfully did the wrong thing. Then the employer delivered the consequences of his actions, *"Take the money from this servant, and give it to the one with the ten bags of silver. To those who use well what they are given, even more will be given, and they will have an abundance. But from those who do nothing, even what little they have will be taken away"* (Matthew 25:28-29). His master punished him not for what he did, but for what he had failed to do.

You might be thinking that the punishment was too harsh. After all, the master didn't lose anything. How about looking at this same incident from another perspective? God has placed certain talents and abilities in you. You have the opportunity to use these special talents in ministry. Now I'm not thinking about special skills and abilities. It could be something simple like cleaning the church, volunteering in a homeless shelter or helping in the nursery at church. If God gave you the opportunity to serve, you should not neglect your duty. That neglect of duty would be sin. The neglect is not based on ability but on availability.

Esther's Choice

The Book of Esther describes a great crisis when the Jews were threatened with slaughter and their fate was in the hands of the Persian king. When Queen Vashti, the Persian queen, lost her position by insulting the king, King Xerxes chose Esther a Jewess to replace her. The king's Chief Minister Haman, who was the most powerful man in the empire, hated Esther's uncle Mordecai because Mordecai refused to bow down before him. Haman devised a plan to kill all the Jews in the province because he wanted to destroy this man Mordecai.

When Mordecai heard the news, he went into mourning. He dressed in garments designated for mourning and went about weeping loudly in the streets. When the other Jews were made aware of the impending slaughter, they, too, were mourning. Queen Esther, Mordecai's niece was isolated in the palace and was not aware of what was happening.

Mordecai then sent Esther a copy of the decree which stated the date of the slaughter. He also asked her to speak to the king on their behalf. Initially Esther refused. Mordecai informed her that she had the privileged position of speaking to the king. He reminded her of her Jewish heritage and warned her that her palace retreat would not exempt her from what would happen to the Jews in the kingdom. She was in a position to gain access to the king but if she was reluctant to do so Mordecai explained that, with or without her help, God would send deliverance to them. But, if she refused to do what was right, she and her family could lose their lives.

Esther now had to examine herself. She realized that God had given her the opportunity to be queen in the kingdom for such a time as this. If she neglected her duty to God and her people, she would pay a high price. Many times in life, people have the same choice to make. It's easy to say, "No, I can't be bothered; ask someone else." God expects His children to what is right whether it involves pleasure or pain.

Esther finally decided that she would do what was right. She went before the king and exposed the plot of Haman. As a result, Haman and his sons were executed. However, according to Persian law, the decree that had already gone out to slaughter the Jews could not be withdrawn. But the king was able to issue a second decree permitting Esther's people to defend themselves against the attack that Haman had planned, and the king signed this decree with his seal. The Jews rose up and defended themselves and in the end were delivered because one person chose to do the right thing (Esther 9).

Loving God requires that you do what is right. The employee made a choice to engage in irresponsible behavior. His employer was aware that his actions were those of willful neglect. He made a choice and had to live with the consequences. Esther decided to refrain from doing what was right. Fortunately, she had Mordecai to point out the error of her ways. Everyone needs a Mordecai to set them on the right path when they are neglectful of their duty.

Sometimes you have to make some difficult decisions. Oftentimes, doing what is right makes you look stupid and weak. Society has traveled down a path that replaces doing what is right with doing what feels good. What do you do when doing what is right does not make you happy? Do it anyway. Loving God means doing what is right. Love does what is right.

Life Application

Do you struggle with doing what is right? What are some of the issues you struggle with? Make a list.

Action Step

Take a close look at your list. Choose the item you consider most important and develop a plan to do what is right. Read James 4:17 daily to help develop the principle of doing what is right.

Read and meditate on:

Esther 2: 8-20; 3:1-12; 4:1-17; 5:1-4; 7:1-10; 8:3-8; Matthew 7:24-27; 25:14-30; Romans 12:20-21; Colossians 3:14-17; 1 John 3:7-10; Isaiah 1:10-17

The Word in My Life

I learned: _____

_____

Adjustments I can make: _____

_____

Prayer

Father, forgive me for neglecting to do what is right because my neglect is sin. Lord, I confess that I am influenced by what looks good instead of what's right. Going forward, help me to do what is right, in Jesus' name, Amen.

Thought for the Day

I am responsible for my actions.

Nine

LOVE IS OUR LOGO

"Teach these new disciples to obey all the commands I have given you. And be sure of this: I am with you always, even to the end of the age."

(Matthew 28:20)

Every organization has its own rules and regulations. When you are at work, you have to follow the policies of the organization that employs you. If you join a sports team for recreation, you have to abide by their policies. While Jesus was on the earth, He set definite guidelines for His disciples to follow. When He was about to ascend to heaven, He left the disciples with a mandate: they had to teach the new disciples all the commands He gave them.

Why are guidelines and commands important? They become your brand. Every brand has a logo. In the body of Christ love is the logo; it is represented by the cross.

Businesses use logos to draw attention to their products and services. Sometimes, the logo takes on a life of its own. Before a child can speak, they can recognize the golden arches of McDonalds' logo. McDonalds have also built in some things to engage their target audience like Ronald McDonald or the toy in a happy meal. Their target audience may not work or have money; but they are connected to individuals who have money. Yet, McDonalds is the most famous fast food chain even though they target an audience who is unemployed. If you don't believe me, put a two year old in your car and drive around; you might have to stop and buy a happy meal.

Your logo is an identity point; it's the important component in your identity just like an organization. Ronald McDonald and happy meal toys are great but it's the golden arches that bring parents with their children in to the restaurant. People of faith have a logo and the logo is love. There are people who give large sums of money to do charitable endeavors and those activities are great. But that does not necessarily fulfill the criteria of the logo.

Moved by Compassion

Jesus demonstrated love in every area of His life to those He met. In Luke chapter 7, Jesus was on His way to Nain and a huge crowd followed Him. As He was about to enter the village, He met a funeral procession going out. A widow was on her way to bury her only son. *"When the Lord saw her, his heart overflowed with compassion. "Don't cry!" he said"* (Luke 7: 13). Jesus went up to the bier, and spoke words of life into his dead body, and the young man sat up. He brought joy into the widow's life.

This was not an isolated incident. There were many individuals that Jesus met that caused His heart to overflow with compassion. This compassion was not human compassion that expresses a concern for the misfortune of others. It was a compassion rooted in love that went beyond concern and sympathy and turned to action. It made a huge change in the life of the individual.

In Matthew 20, Jesus was leaving Jericho when two blind men heard that He was in the vicinity. They had heard about His Love Walk. He loved people and would never turn away anyone in need. The blind men couldn't tell where He was exactly, so they cried out to Him with raised voices. The crowd didn't care about them and told them to be quiet. This made them yell out to Him even louder and Jesus heard them. When Jesus saw their condition, He stopped. Jesus, would never allow someone who is sick and suffering, or in their case blind, to leave His presence unchanged. He took the time; touched their eyes and they received their sight.

Jesus demonstrated love to all He met and was not influenced by what the crowd said or thought. His love superseded the opinions of the crowd or religious folk. The religious crowd cared about the law, not the people. In Matthew 12, Jesus chose to demonstrate His love for man by transcending the religious law. He saw a man with a deformed hand. These religious folk anxiously awaited His response so they could accuse Him of breaking the Sabbath. But Jesus knew their thoughts and asked them what would they do if their sheep fell into a well on the Sabbath? They could not reply because Jesus exposed the condition of their heart and their Love Walk. Theirs was governed by the law when it was convenient to obey. But Jesus had compassion and healed the man's hand regardless of what day it was.

Jesus didn't show love only when it was convenient, He demonstrated love during the most difficult moments in His life. When His time on earth was coming to an end, Jesus was in the garden of Gethsemane for a time of prayer. The religious leaders arrived with a crowd to arrest Him. Peter drew his sword and took off the ear of one of the men. To this, Jesus responded, *"'No more of this.' And he touched the man's ear and healed him"* (Luke 22:51). His Love Walk didn't change even if He was arrested. *"Then the people who had arrested Jesus led him to the home of Caiaphas, the high priest, where the teachers of religious law and the elders had gathered"* (Matthew 26:57).

The Sanhedrin Council, consisting of the Sadducees and Pharisees, came together because they wanted to silence His message. Jesus was not afraid of them because He placed the well-being of the individual above the law. They had the authority to enforce religious laws and penalties but, since they wanted him dead, they needed the authority of Rome. They devised a plan that would be approved of by the Roman rulers so that Jesus could be found guilty of a crime against Rome and be put to death. Pilate could find no fault with Him but the crowd decided that He should die. To appease the mob, Pilate ordered Him to be crucified. Two thieves were crucified with Him, one on the left and one on the right.

While He hung on the cross, Jesus was motivated by love. One of the crucified men decided to join with the crowd and mock Him. The other individual recognized there was something different in Jesus. He asked Jesus to remember him and Jesus said, *"I assure you, today you will be with me in paradise"* (Luke 23:43). He had compassion on Mary, His mother, so He transferred the care of her to John, His disciple. John cared for her like his own mother. And His last breath on the cross was an appeal to the Father to forgive those responsible for His death, *"Father, forgive them, for they don't know what they are doing"* (Luke 23:24).

Jesus demonstrated His love through His conduct. Love defined His brand. His love drove Him to action. He did not discriminate; He took time for everyone. He loved those who accepted Him and He also loved those who hated Him and everything He stood for. Jesus didn't leave the message of love in a manifesto for people to decipher what it means: He demonstrated it with His very life. Love is His brand and He led by example. Jesus' entire life was a Love Walk.

There is probably no greater comfort in the time of difficulty than knowing you are not alone. In our lives when difficulties arise, many of those around you head for the exit door. But Jesus left words of encouragement with His followers, asking them to instruct those who would join the disciples' team that they were not alone.

When you face difficult moments in your life, as a disciple, you, too, are not alone. He is with you. And Jesus takes it one step further, He sends people into your life to help you. So it's not if, but when, you go through difficult times, be encouraged; you have all the power of heaven at your disposal so that you can walk in victory.

Jesus knew the importance of the Love Walk. He said, *"Your love for one another will prove to the world that you are my disciples"* (John 13:35). He didn't say "...by the miracles you do," or "by the sermons you preach" but "by the way you love." Love is our logo.

Life Application

The world says, "Love those who love you and hate those who hate you." Jesus said, "Love your neighbor as yourself." Why is it important to love your neighbor as yourself?

Action Step

When you decide to change your Love Walk, there will be challenges. Choose one thing in your life to change your walk. List two things you can do so that you can be successful.

Read and meditate on:

Matthew 12:8-13; 20:29-34; 26:57-68; 27:11-26; Luke 7; 20:47-53; 23:26-43; John 15:9-17; 19:26-27; Ephesians 5:21-33; Colossians 3:15-15; James 1:22

The Word in My Life

I learned: _____

_____

Adjustments I can make: _____

_____

Prayer

Father, I thank You for sending Jesus to be the example of love in the world. Love is our logo and I want to represent You well. Help me to love through all the circumstances of my life so that others can see Christ in me, in Jesus' name, Amen.

Thought for the Day

I will be known for my Love Walk.

Ten

LOVE: THE CHOICEST GRACE

Three things will last forever — faith, hope, and love — and the greatest of these is love.

(1 Corinthians 13:13)

*T*his same verse in the Amplified Version says, *"And now there remain: faith [abiding trust in God and His promises], hope [confident expectation of eternal salvation], love [unselfish love for others growing out of God's love for me], these three [the choicest graces]; but the greatest of these is love."*

There is no greater force on this earth than love. The Bible tells us, *"For God so loved the world that He gave His only begotten Son, that whoever believes in Him should not perish but have everlasting life"* (John 3:16 NKJV). The God of the universe loves mankind to such a great extent that He gave. He didn't give something of little or no value: He gave His best.

The Apostle Paul, called love the choicest grace. You see, you can do great feats without love but you can't love without action. Society places great importance on the accomplishments of the mighty. They do great deeds even if they are disrespectful to their employees and those around them. Yet society throws accolades at them because they value their accomplishments above their character.

Giving One's Best

Many times, simple folk give in greater measure than those with means. One day, Jesus wanted to teach His disciples on giving. He was sitting near the collection box and observed people of means come and deposit large amounts. Then a widow woman came by and gave two small coins. Jesus explained that the widow gave more than the others, although her contribution was so minute. The others gave a small portion of their abundance, while she gave all she had (Mark 12:41-44). There are many people like her today who give their all. These simple folk, deemed unimportant by society, give beyond their capacity. They feed the hungry, clothe the naked and love the unlovable. They are the people society views as weak because it does not understand their Love Walk.

When you look in the book of Acts you find a young man, Stephen, who gave his best. In chapter 6 of Acts, the Apostles needed help to ensure that the daily activities of the church could run smoothly, so they chose seven men of good report. They gave these men the responsibility of taking care of the members in need; it takes genuine love to administer care to people in need. The first name mentioned was Stephen.

Stephen not only performed his duties wholeheartedly but demonstrated the life of the Holy Spirit in him. That angered the religious Jews. You would think the religious folk of his time would applaud his actions. But they didn't. In fact, *"None of them could stand against the wisdom and the Spirit with which Stephen spoke"* (Acts 6:10). They wanted to silence Stephen, in his words and his actions. Unable to find fault with Stephen's life or his work, they made up a lie. The Jews arrested Stephen and, at the court hearing he delivered an eloquent rebuttal of their false statements and lashed out at them for their persecution of the prophets in every generation. His words pricked their hearts. They responded by dragging him outside of the city, stoning him to death.

Their actions did nothing to change Stephen's compassion for them. While he lay dying, he prayed for them. He didn't call them murderers or ask God to take revenge on them; instead he asked God to forgive them. *"Lord, don't charge them with this sin!"*(Acts 7:60) He demonstrated the love of God with his dying breath.

Love is the choicest grace. Everything you do is a response to your love for God. The Bible teaches, *"For when we place our faith in Christ Jesus, there is no benefit in being circumcised or being uncircumcised. What is important is faith expressing itself in love"* (Galatians 5:6). In their culture, those issues were important. Now, people are concerned about prestige and accolades. Those are great but are of little consequence in your Love Walk. You cannot go to a university and follow a course of study to learn how to love. This love comes from the Holy Spirit working in your life, *"But the Holy Spirit produces this kind of fruit in our lives: love, joy, peace, patience, kindness, goodness, faithfulness"* (Galatians 5:22-23).

This choicest grace fulfills the law. As Romans 13:10 says, *"Love does no wrong to others, so love fulfills the requirements of God's law."* When Moses went up to the mountain, God gave him the Ten Commandments, also called the Law. Now Exodus 20:17 says, *"You must not covet your neighbor's house. You must not covet your neighbor's wife, male or female servant, ox or donkey, or anything else that belongs to your neighbor."* The most important word in the verse is 'covet:' it means to desire wrongfully. When you desire things that belong to your neighbor, you might engage in inappropriate activities in order to gain these items; you might even harm your neighbor. Love fulfills the law. Jesus best summed it up:

"'And you must love the LORD your God with all your heart, all your soul, all your mind, and all your strength.' The second is equally important: 'Love your neighbor as yourself.' No other commandment is greater than these" (Mark 12:30-31).

Who is my Neighbor?

The notion of who was one's neighbor confused many in Jesus' day and I believe some are still struggling to identify their neighbor. To demonstrate how to recognize a neighbor, Jesus told a parable to an expert in the law (Luke 10:25-37). This expert understood that love fulfills the law but he wanted to trick Jesus. In His parable, Jesus describes how a man traveling alone was robbed and left for dead. While he lay helpless, a priest walked by, saw the man and crossed over on the other side. A Levite passed by and he, too, crossed over on the other side. But a Samaritan passed by, administered first aid then took the wounded man to a care facility, paid for his care and promised to return and reimburse the provider if the services exceeded the estimated cost. Then Jesus asked the expert to identify the individual who was a neighbor to the wounded man. The expert identified the Samaritan. This was a powerful example of love. It showed how, in spite of the Jews' and Samaritans' hatred for each other, an enemy stopped and gave care. This is contrasted with the religious members of his own community who abandoned the helpless man. The Samaritan demonstrated his Love Walk.

James also knew the importance of the Love Walk. *"Yes indeed, it is good when you obey the royal law as found in the Scriptures: 'Love your neighbor as yourself'"* (James 2:8). It's important to love yourself but it's just as important to apply the same degree of love to your neighbor.

Sometimes, your Love Walk can be the most difficult walk in your life. You have to constantly evaluate and redirect yourself lest you find yourself walking according to your own standards and not those set by God. As with any walk, there will be pitfalls along the way. You will at times stumble and fall. Don't let that setback derail your walk. As long as there is life, there is the opportunity to correct the error and continue on your walk. In so doing, your Love Walk will demonstrate to the world that you are a disciple. Love is the choicest grace.

Life Application

You thought that you expressed love in a manner that demonstrated love as the choicest grace. Now you are not so sure. What are some changes you can make to love in a manner that pleases God?

Action Step

You want to start anew and you are not sure where to begin. Stephen's Love Walk came out of a relationship with God. What is your first step? Use your quiet time to develop your Love Walk.

Read and meditate on:

Matthew 5:43-48; Mark 12:28-34; Mark 41-44; Luke 10:25-37; Acts 6:8-15; Acts 7:51-60; Romans 13:8-10; 1 Corinthians 13:1-13; Galatians 5:2-6; 22-23; James 2:8-11

The Word in My Life

I learned: _____

_____

Adjustments I can make: _____

_____

Prayer

Father, I want to walk in love from a heart filled with Your love. Jesus demonstrated love when He forgave the thief on the cross. I want to demonstrate that kind of love in my life. Help me to love like You love, in Jesus' name, Amen.

Thought for the Day

I will walk in love.

EPILOGUE

The Love Walk is not a sprint. It is a long distance challenge. The Bible says, *"The fastest runner doesn't always win the race, and the strongest warrior doesn't always win the battle"* (Ecclesiastes 9:11). In order to complete the challenge you have to remain on track.

As you continue in your walk, sometimes the terrain is smooth and it makes the walk easy; at other times, the walk is uphill. In life just as there are added benefits of walking uphill, the same is true for the Love Walk. You will reap greater benefits for those uphill battles.

The most important thing to remember is that you are not alone. When the going gets tough, your help is in God. God will help you to persevere in your Love Walk when your human ability fails. Love never fails!

Claudette Glaude-Scott

FROM
PRISON
TO PALACE

Overcoming Challenges
and Rising to the Top

About The Author

Claudette is a writer and woman of God who enjoys helping others. Her life of faith has been greatly influenced by her late grandmother, an amazing woman of God, who imparted the joy of loving the Lord and serving others.

Everyone lives life with a unique purpose from God, and it has been so fulfilling to Claudette to know that her purpose is to make a difference. There were challenges along the way, but she braved them all and learnt from them, and it was from here that another ministry opened up for her.

Her first book *From Prison to Palace: Overcoming Challenges and rising to The Top* was published in 2018. Claudette hopes that people learn from her life and understand that life is all about challenges: it's from these challenges that we gain our freedom and victory.

It has been a rich journey so far, and she hopes to continue in her Love Walk and expand her ministries.

Made in the USA
Las Vegas, NV
29 March 2024

87987793R00059